Team Goon

THIS IS A 5.5 X 8.5 110 PAGE JOURNAL/DIARY TO USE AS YOU WISH.

100 PLUS LINED PAGES TO TAKE NOTES, WRITE STORIES, USE AS A DIARY OR WHATEVER YOU CAN THINK OF.

IT'S TIME TO HAVE FUN AND BE CREATIVE.

TEAM GOON JOURNAL

FIRST EDITION

ISBN: 9781549751097
INDEPENDENTLY PUBLISHED

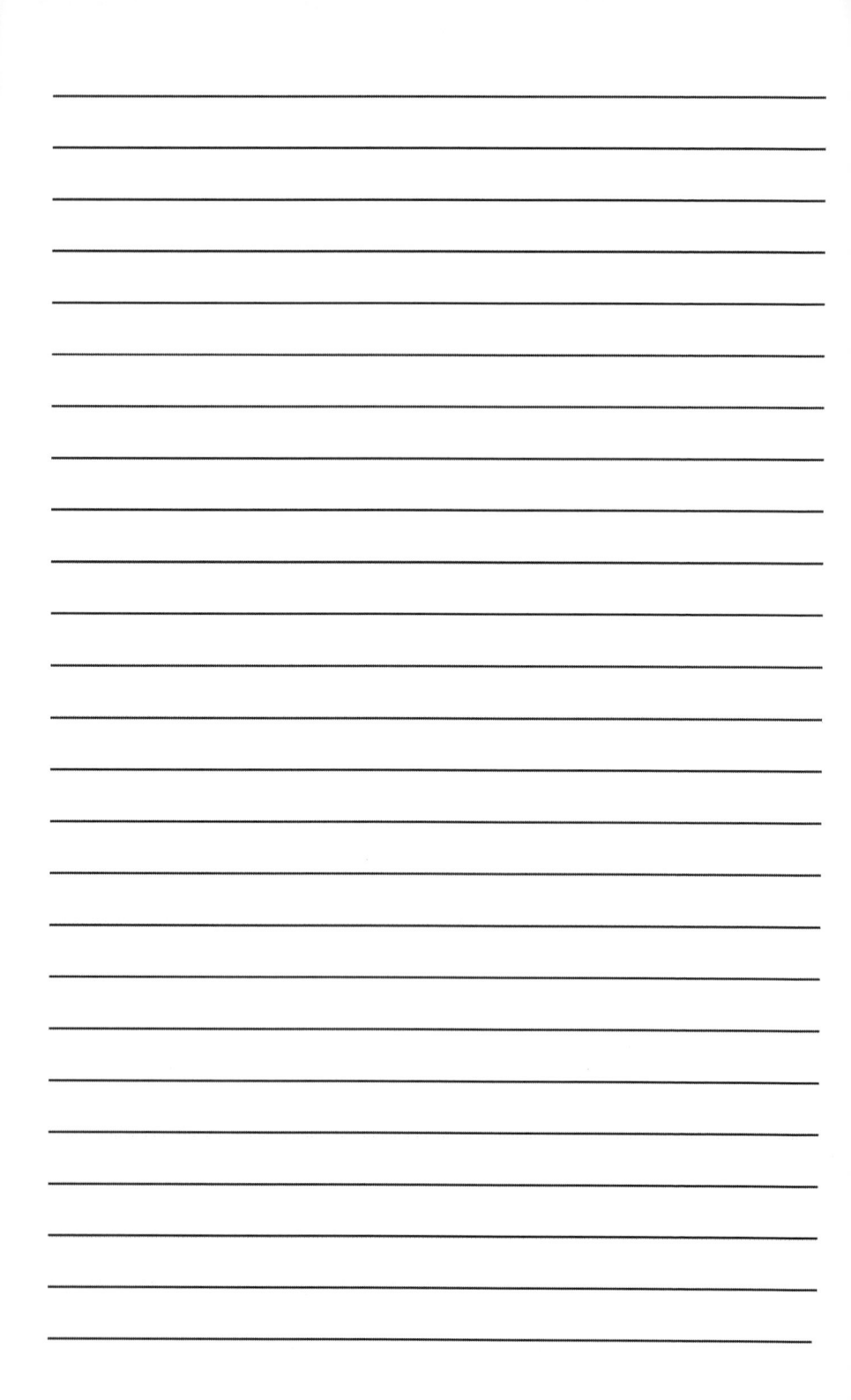

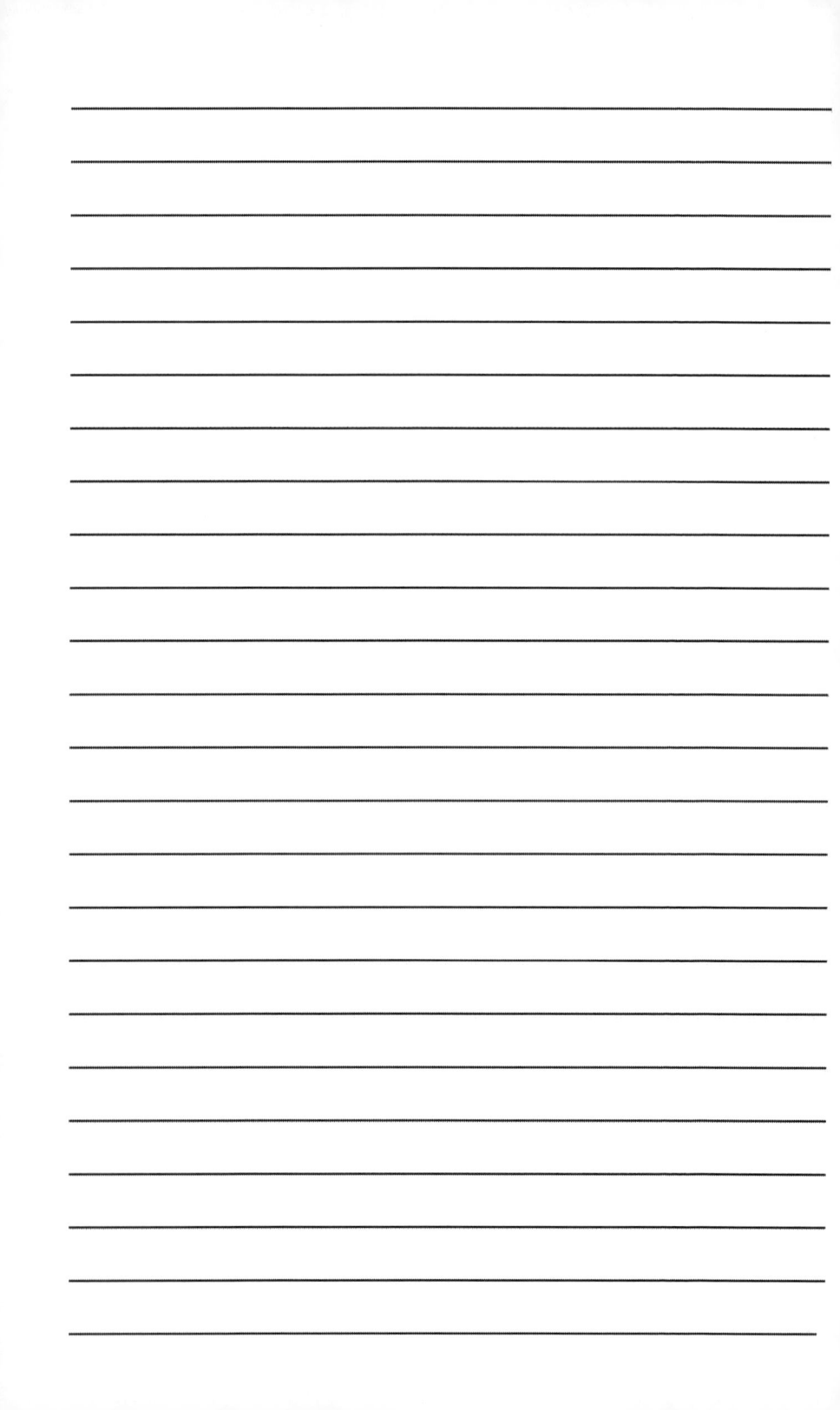

Do you have secrets you need to protect?

You may also be interested or know someone who would enjoy our other journals

I Believe in Unicorns

I Believe in Bigfoot

I Believe in Angels

I Believe in Love

I Believe in Aliens

I Believe in Superheroes

I Believe in Dragons

My Own Joke Journal

Superhero Secrets

And Many More....

I HOPE YOU ENJOY THIS JOURNAL.

MANY MORE I BELIEVE JOURNALS AND OTHER OPTIONS ARE AVAILABLE AT:

niftyjournals.com

#WRITE
#CREATE
#ILLUSTRATE

THANK YOU FOR YOUR PURCHASE

25759762R00061

Printed in Great Britain
by Amazon